AGE 13-14
Key Stage 3

national TESTS practice papers

FOR THE YEAR 2002

Key Stage 3
Maths Book 2

practice Papers

Contents	Page
Introduction – notes for parents	
The National Tests: A Summary	iii
Maths at Key Stage 3	iv
Paper 1 (non-calculator)	1
Paper 2 (calculator)	24
Mental Maths Test	43
Answers	
Paper 1	48
Paper 2	52
Mental Maths Test	56
National Curriculum Levels	57
Level 8 Extension Paper	
Paper	58
Answers	60

First published 2001
exclusively for WHSmith by

Hodder & Stoughton Educational,
a division of Hodder Headline Ltd
338 Euston Road
London NW1 3BH

Text © Hodder & Stoughton Educational 2001

All rights reserved. No part of this publication may be reproduced or transmitted in any form or by any means, electronic or mechanical, including photocopying, recording or any information storage and retrieval system, without permission in writing from the publisher.

A CIP record for this book is available from the British Library.

Authors: Steve Mills and Hilary Koll

ISBN 0340 84591 0

Printed and bound by Graphycems, Spain

> NOTE: The tests, questions and advice in this book are not reproductions of the official test materials sent to schools. The official testing process is supported by guidance and training for teachers in setting and marking tests and interpreting the results. The results achieved in the tests in this book may not be the same as are achieved in the official tests.

Introduction

The National Tests: A Summary

What are the National Tests?

Children who attend state schools in England and Wales sit National Tests (commonly known as SATs) at the ages of 7, 11 and 14, usually at the beginning of May. The test results are accompanied by an assessment by the child's teacher (at Key Stage 3 this also covers non-tested subjects such as History or Geography).

The results are used by the school to assess each child's level of knowledge and progress in English and Maths at Key Stage 1 and English, Maths and Science at Key Stages 2 and 3. They also provide guidance for the child's next teacher when he or she is planning the year.

The educational calendar for children aged 5-14 is structured as follows:

Key Stage	Year	Age by end of year	National Test
1 (KS1)	1	6	
	2	7	KEY STAGE 1
	3	8	Optional Year 3
2 (KS2)	4	9	Optional Year 4
	5	10	Optional Year 5
	6	11	KEY STAGE 2
3 (KS3)	7	12	
	8	13	
	9	14	KEY STAGE 3

Timetable

Key Stage 3 students will sit their tests on **7–13 May 2002**, with the following timetable (check with the school as dates may change):

Levels

National targets have been set for children's results in the National Tests, as follows:

LEVEL	AGE 7	AGE 11	AGE 14
8			
7			
6			
5			
4			
3			
2			
2a			
2b			
2c			
1			

Below expected level · Above expected level
Expected level · Exceptional

What can parents do to help?

While it is never a good idea to encourage cramming, you can help your child to succeed by:

- Making sure he or she has enough food, sleep and leisure time during the test period.
- Practising important skills such as writing, spelling and mental arithmetic.
- Telling him or her what to expect in the test, such as important symbols.
- Helping him or her to be comfortable in test conditions including working within a time limit, reading questions carefully and understanding different ways of answering.

Tuesday 7 May	Wednesday 8 May	Thursday 9 May	Friday 10 May	Monday 13 May
		MORNING		
English Paper 1 ($1\frac{1}{2}$ hours plus 15 minutes reading time)	Mathematics Paper 1 (1 hour)	English Extension Paper ($1\frac{1}{2}$ hours)	Science Paper 1 (1 hour)	Science Extension Paper (1 hour)
	Mental Arithmetic Tests A and C (20 minutes)	Mental Arithmetic Test B (20 minutes)		
		AFTERNOON		
English Paper 2 ($1\frac{1}{4}$ hours)	Mathematics Paper 2 (1 hour)	Mathematics Extension Paper (1 hour)	Science Paper 2 (1 hour)	

Introduction
Maths at Key Stage 3

The Key stage 3 Maths test consists of two written papers, one to be taken without a calculator and the other with a calculator, and a mental arithmetic test. The tests will cover aspects of Number and Algebra, Shape, Space and Measures and Handling Data.

Levels and tiers of entry

For mathematics, your child will be entered for one of four tiers. Your child's teacher will make a judgement about which of the tiers to enter your child for, deciding on the tier that best matches his or her ability.

Tiers: Levels 3–5
         Levels 4–6
         Levels 5–7
         Levels 6–8.

An additional extension paper can be taken by children working at level 8 or beyond.

This book includes two written papers that cover the most popular tiers of entry. Paper 1 covers levels 4–6 and Paper 2 covers levels 5–7. Separate level 8 practice questions are included for those performing above the expected standard for 14-year-olds. The mental arithmetic test includes questions at levels 4–7.

To gain an idea of the level at which your child is working, use the table on page 57, which shows you how to convert your child's marks into a National Curriculum level.

Setting the Maths Tests

Equipment needed

Paper 1: pen, pencil, ruler, rubber,

Paper 2: pen, pencil, ruler, rubber, protractor or angle measurer, pair of compasses, scientific or graphic calculator, tracing paper, mirror (optional).

Mental Maths Test: pencil and rubber.

A clock or watch with a second hand is useful for ensuring times for each question on the mental test are appropriate. No extra paper is needed. Answers and working are written in this book.

The written papers

A formula sheet is included for each test. Encourage your child to refer to it where necessary. Each written paper lasts for **1 hour**, starting with easier questions and gradually becoming more difficult.

The mental maths test

The mental test should take approximately **20 minutes** to give. Cut out pages 43 to 44 so you can read them aloud to your child.

You will need to ensure that you read the questions to your child within the set times. Read each question twice. Your child should use the sheets on pages 45, 46 and 47 to write his or her answers.

1 mark should be awarded for each correct answer.

Marking the tests

Next to each question in the written tests is a number indicating how many marks the question or part of the question is worth.

Enter your child's mark into the circle above, using the answer pages to help you decide how many points to award.

The answer pages (48 to 56) also offer advice, provide information about common errors made by pupils and include tips to help your child understand the mathematical ideas.

Find your child's total score from the written papers and refer to page 57 for information about the level at which your child might be working.

Whatever your child achieves, help him or her to feel positive and confident by giving plenty of praise for the efforts made.

Paper 1
Non-Calculator Paper

You *cannot* use a calculator for any questions in Paper 1.

Formulae

You might need to use these formulae.

AREA

Circle

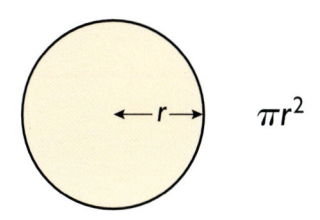

πr^2

Take π as 3.14.

Triangle

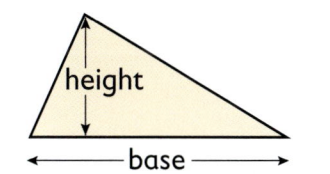

$\dfrac{\text{base} \times \text{height}}{2}$

Parallelogram

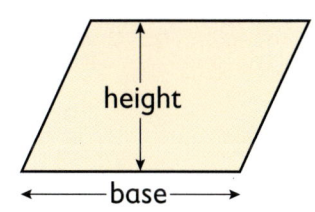

base × height

Trapezium

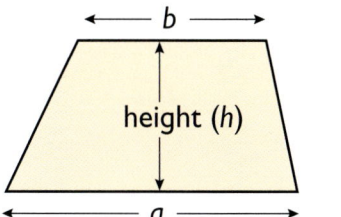

$\dfrac{(a + b)}{2} \times h$

LENGTH

Circle

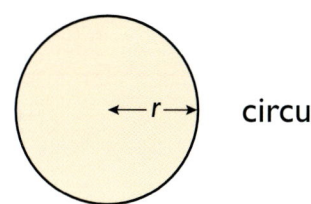

circumference = $2\pi r$

VOLUME

Prism

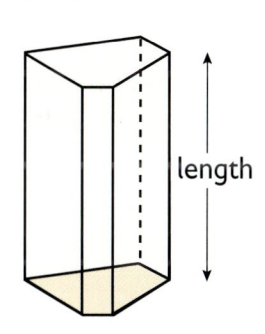

area of cross section × length

You will need:
pen, pencil, rubber, ruler.

1

Paper 1

Practice questions

Example

What fraction of this bar of chocolate has been eaten?

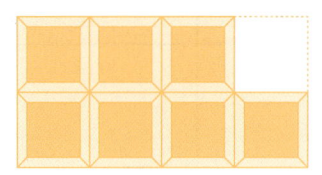

$$\frac{1}{8}$$

a What fraction of this bar of chocolate has been eaten?

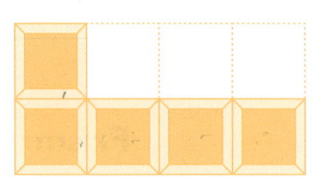

$\frac{5}{8}$

b What fraction of this bar of chocolate has been eaten? Give your answer in its simplest form.

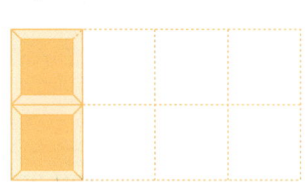

$\frac{2}{8} = \frac{1}{4}$

Paper 1

Fractions and percentages

1 $\frac{1}{2}$ of this bar of chocolate has been eaten.

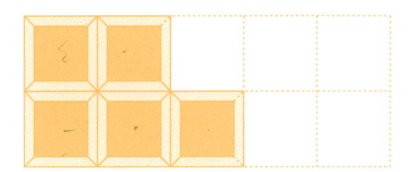

a What fraction of this bar of chocolate has been eaten?

$\frac{7}{10}$

1

b What fraction of this bar of chocolate has been eaten? Give your answer in its simplest form.

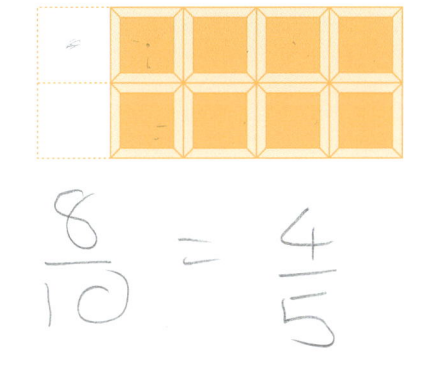

$\frac{8}{10} = \frac{4}{5}$

1

What percentage of the bar has not been eaten?

20%

1

TOTAL 3

3

Paper 1

c Shade $\frac{3}{5}$ of this chocolate bar.

d Shade **30%** of the chocolate bar below.

Paper 1

Money

2 Nita goes to the ice rink with two friends.

She buys **three** tickets that are all the same price.

She pays with a **£10 note** and is given **£2.50 change**.

a How much does **one** ticket cost?

1

b Tickets to watch the Ice Show cost **£3.20**.

How much would **6** tickets cost?

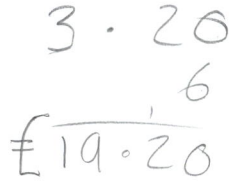

3 . 20
    6
£19.20

1

c Mr Farrell spends exactly **£64** on tickets for the Ice Show for some children.

How many tickets does he buy?

1

TOTAL

3

5

Paper 1

Tiles

3 These are tiles on a bathroom wall.

a Colour **4 more tiles** so that the thick line is **a line of symmetry**.

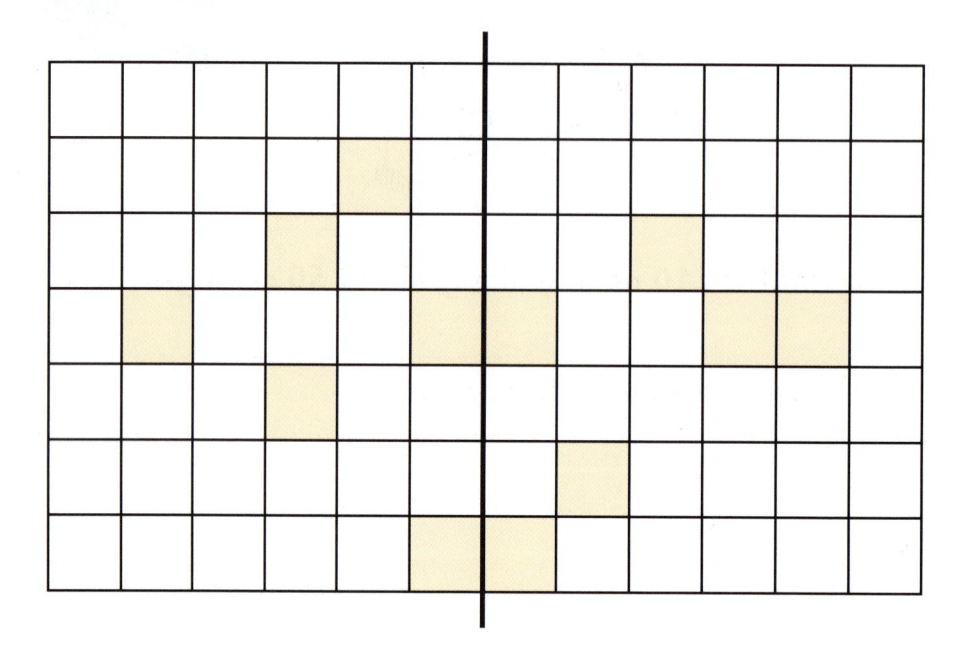

b Colour **5 more tiles** so that the thick line is **a line of symmetry**.

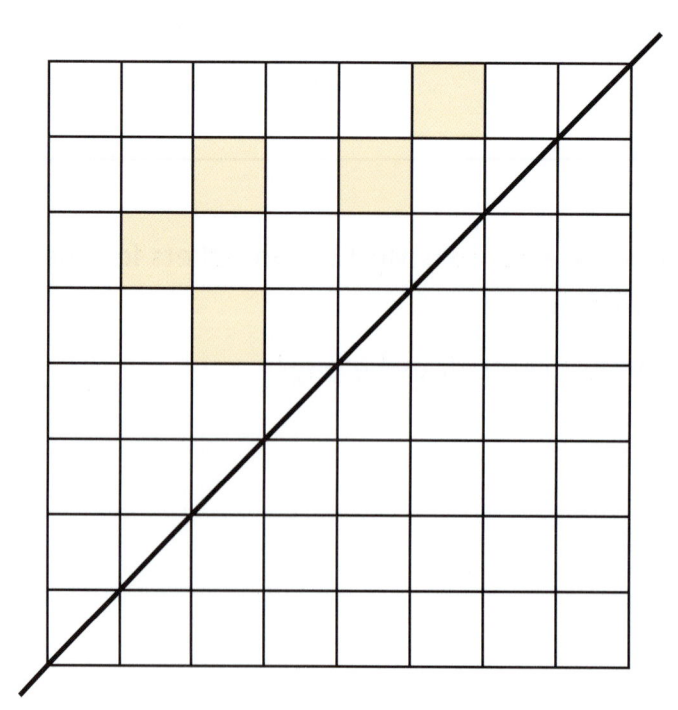

Paper 1

c Colour **12 more tiles** so that both thick lines are **lines of symmetry**.

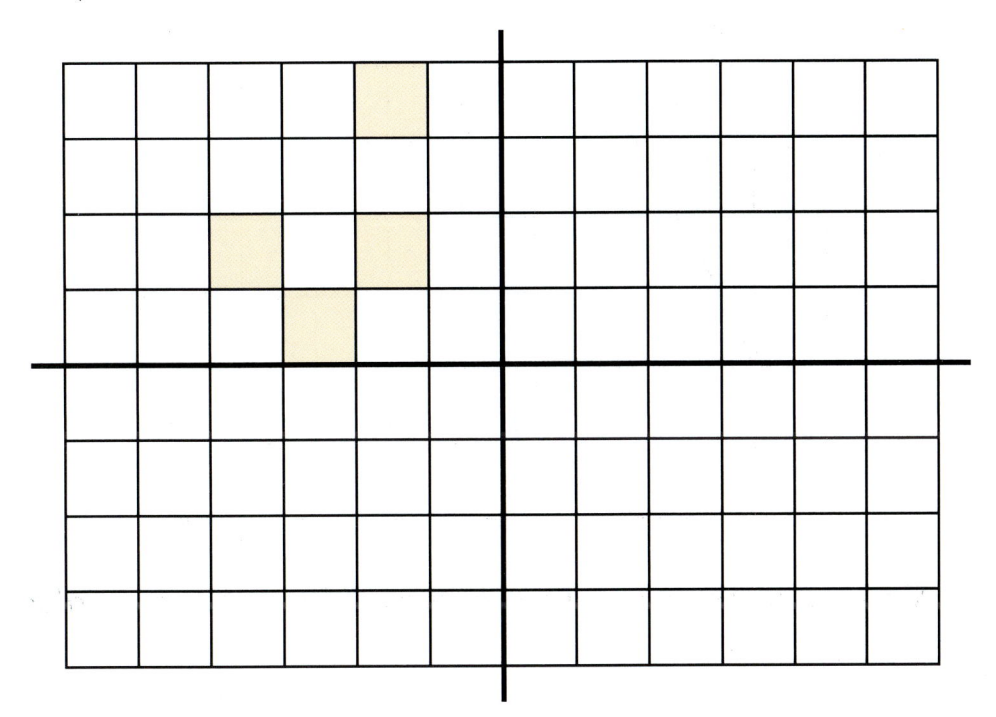

Paper 1

Co-ordinates

4 Shape A has six vertices (corners).

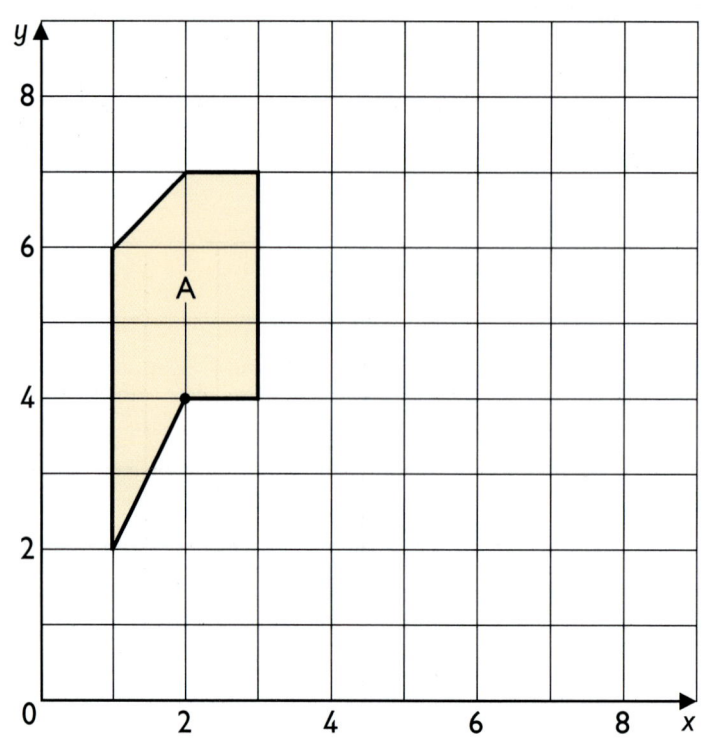

a Write the co-ordinates of the vertices of Shape A in any order.

(1, 2) (,) (,) (,) (,) (,)

Li has thought of a rule to change the co-ordinates of Shape A.

*I will **add 3** to each of the **x co-ordinates***

b Rewrite the co-ordinates, following Li's rule.

(4, 2) (,) (,) (,) (,) (,)

Now mark the new co-ordinates you have written onto the grid and join them up to make a new shape. Label this shape 'B'.

c Explain how Shape A has been changed to Shape B in your own words.

....

....

....

Li has thought of a different rule to change the co-ordinates of a shape.

*I will **subtract 2** from each of the y co-ordinates.*

d Explain how the shape would be changed if Li's new rule was followed.

....

....

....

Paper 1

Missing numbers

5   Write one number in each box to make each equation correct.

a   1030 ÷ ☐ = 103

b   180 ÷ ☐ = 45

c   ☐ − 50 = 92

d   ☐ × 6 = 240

e   ☐ ÷ 6 = 12

6 Nagajan has been doing some multiplying.

This is how he multiplies **17** by **34**.

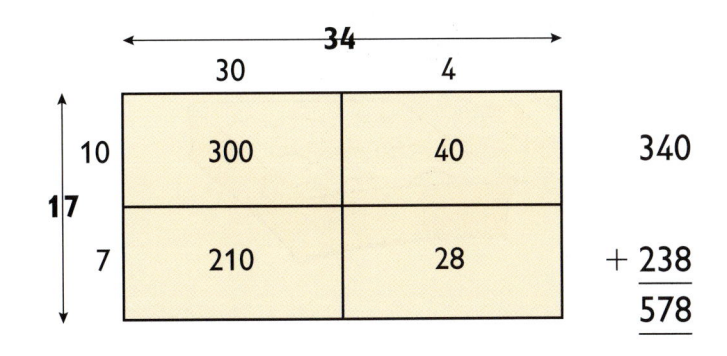

	30	4	
10	300	40	340
7	210	28	+ 238
			578

Use Nagajan's method to find the area of a rectangle **16 cm** by **23 cm**.

Area of rectangle = ... cm^2

Paper 1

Chocolate box

7 A box of chocolates has three types of chocolate: **milk, white** and **dark**.

There are **10 milk, 5 white** and **15 dark** chocolates in a box. Larissa picks a chocolate from a full box without looking.

a What is the **probability** that she picks a **dark** chocolate? Write your answer as a **fraction** in its simplest form.

b Draw a cross on this line to show the probability that Larissa picks a **white** chocolate.

impossible | | | | | | | certain

c Draw a cross on this line to show the probability that Larissa does not pick a **milk** chocolate.

impossible | | | | | | | certain

12

The **first** chocolate Larissa picked was a **dark** chocolate. She eats it.
Larissa now picks a **second** chocolate **from the same box** without looking.

d Tick which of these three statements is true.

   "The next chocolate Larissa picks is likely to be a milk chocolate."

   "The probability of Larissa picking a dark chocolate is the same as before."

   "Larissa is more likely to pick a dark chocolate than any other chocolate."

   Explain your answer.

Paper 1

Film processing

8 In a shop, a machine can process a number of camera films every hour.

Call this number n.

a Write an expression to show how many films the machine can process in **three hours**.

....

b In the shop there is a second machine that takes **twice as long** as the first machine to process films.

Write an expression to show how many films the **second** machine can process in **one hour**.

....

c Write an expression to show the **total** number of films that can be processed by the **two machines** in **one hour**.

....

TOTAL 3

14

Paper 1

Negatives

9 Cathy has cards with some numbers and signs on.

She arranges them to make equations.

Fill in **one** number in **each** equation below.

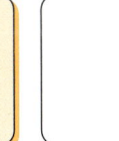

a

⁻3 + ☐ = 5

b

6 − 8 + ☐ = 2

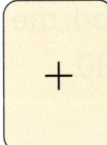

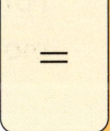

c

5 + ⁻2 + ☐ = ⁻4

d Reorder these cards to give the answer ⁻10.

⁻4   1   ⁻5   +   −

☐ ☐ ☐ ☐ ☐ = ⁻10

1

1

1

1

TOTAL

4

15

Paper 1

Profits

10 This graph shows the monthly profit made by a butcher's shop during a six month period.

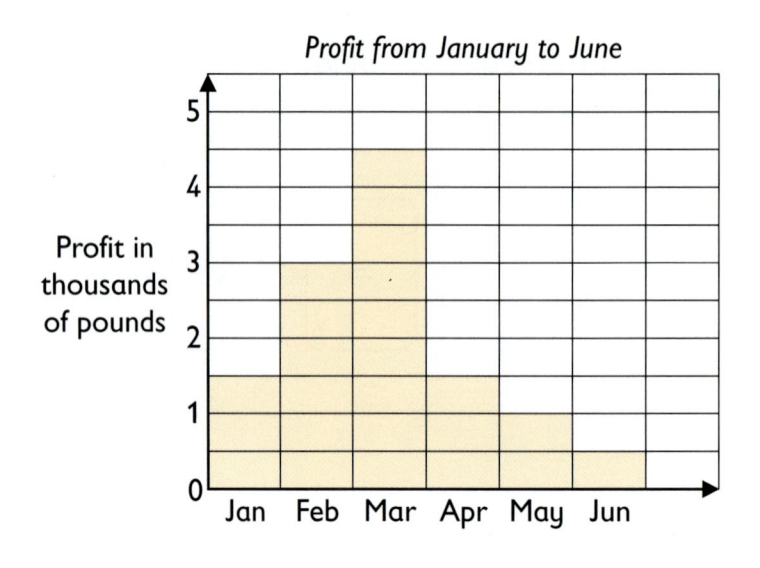

Profit from January to June

Profit in thousands of pounds

Look at the graph.

a Some of the statements below are true and some are false. **Tick** the statements that are **true**.

| For most months during this period, the monthly profit was less than £2000. | |

| For all months during this period, the monthly profit was £1000 or more. | |

| The mean monthly profit during this period was £3000. | |

| The total profit during this period was £12000. | |

b Calculate the **range** of the monthly profits from January to June.

The profits for the following six months (from July to December) were also recorded on a graph.

The **mean** monthly profit for this period was **£1000**.

c Use this information to complete the graph below.

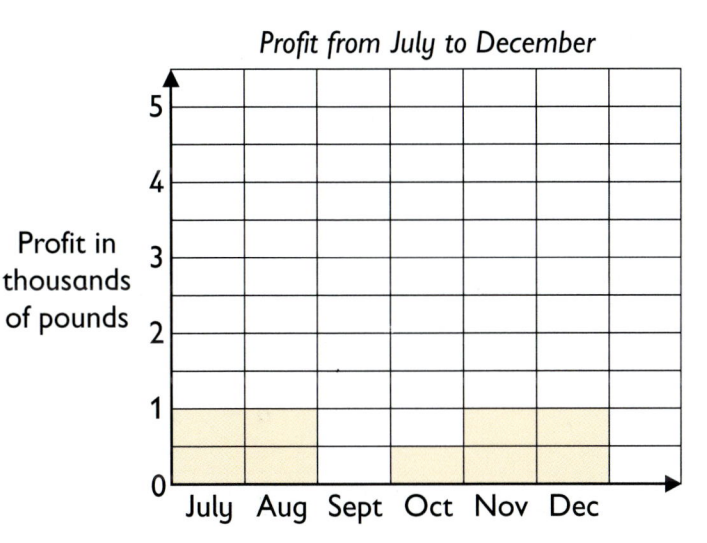

Profit from July to December

Profit in thousands of pounds

d Calculate the mean monthly profit for the **whole year**, from January to December.

Paper 1

Triangles

11 This diagram shows triangle PQR.

Point S lies on the line PQ and point T lies on the line PR.

Line **QR** is parallel to line **ST**.

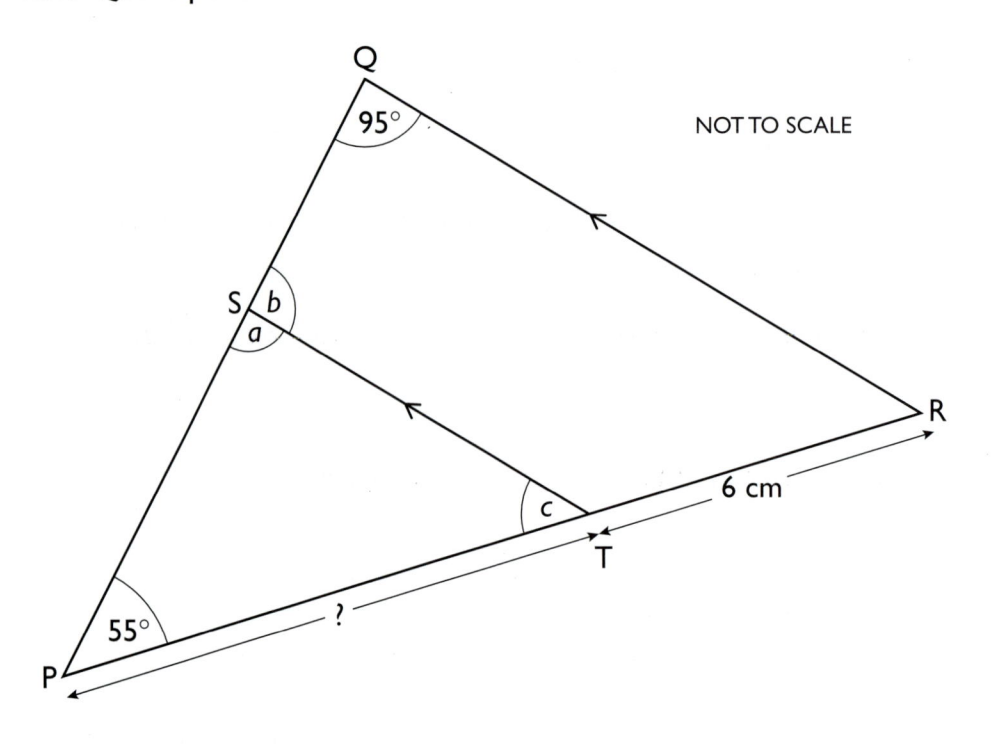

NOT TO SCALE

a Calculate angles *a*, *b* and *c*.

a = ... °

b = ... °

c = ... °

b The sides of triangle PQR are **twice** the length of the sides of triangle PST. The side RT is **6 cm.**

Calculate the length of the line **PT**.

PT = ... cm

3

1

TOTAL

4

18

Paper 1

Sequences

12 Here is part of a number grid made from hexagons. The pattern continues each time by adding a new layer of hexagons along the bottom edge. Each of the hexagons in a layer is numbered.

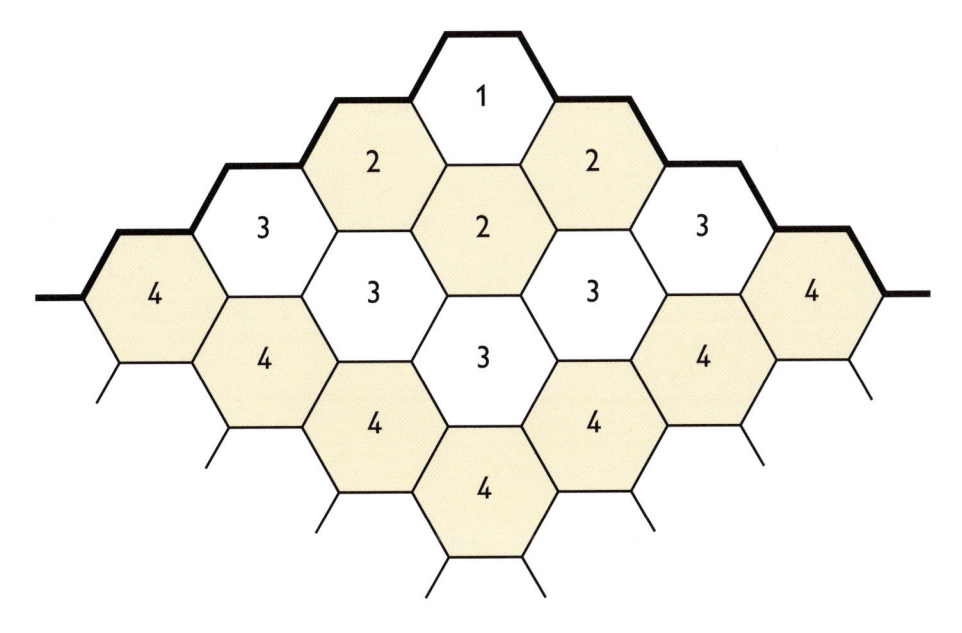

a Calculate how many hexagons will be in layer 6.

b Complete the table.

Layer	1	2	3	4	**10**
Number of hexagons in layer	1	3			

c Write an expression to show the number of hexagons in layer n.

Paper 1

Equations

13 Andrew has been given some equations to solve.

$3x - 10 = 23$ $4y + 20 = 48$ $z^2 - 6 = 58$

a Solve the equations to find the values of x, y and z.

x = ...   y = ...   z = ...

b Andrew solves his equations on a rectangular piece of paper.
The **length** of Andrew's piece of paper is **5 cm more** than the **width**.

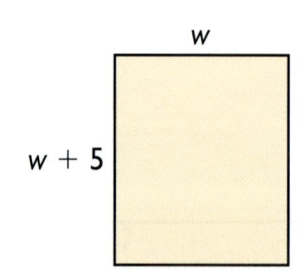

w
w + 5

The **perimeter** of his piece of paper is 110 cm.
Calculate the width of the piece of paper.

14 An author is writing a book with **36 pages.**

This table shows information about how much the author is writing each day.

Day	Number of pages written	Total number of pages written so far	Fraction of book written so far
Monday	2	2	$\frac{1}{18}$
Tuesday	1	3	$\frac{1}{12}$
Wednesday	1	4	
Thursday	8		
Friday	6		
Saturday	9		
Sunday		36	1

a Complete the table so that it shows, for each day,

- the **number of pages written**
- the **total number of pages written**
- the **fraction of the book written**

Give all fractions in their simplest form.

Areas of shapes

15 Here is a trapezium and a triangle joined to make a rectangle.

They are <u>not</u> drawn to scale.

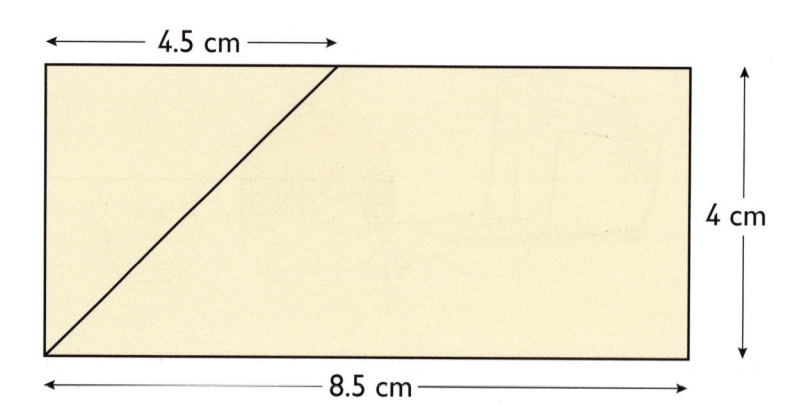

← 4.5 cm →
← 8.5 cm →
4 cm

a Calculate the area of the triangle.

Area of triangle = ... cm²

b Calculate the area of the trapezium.
Show your working.

Area of trapezium = ... cm²

The area of the triangle in the diagram below is **8 cm²**.

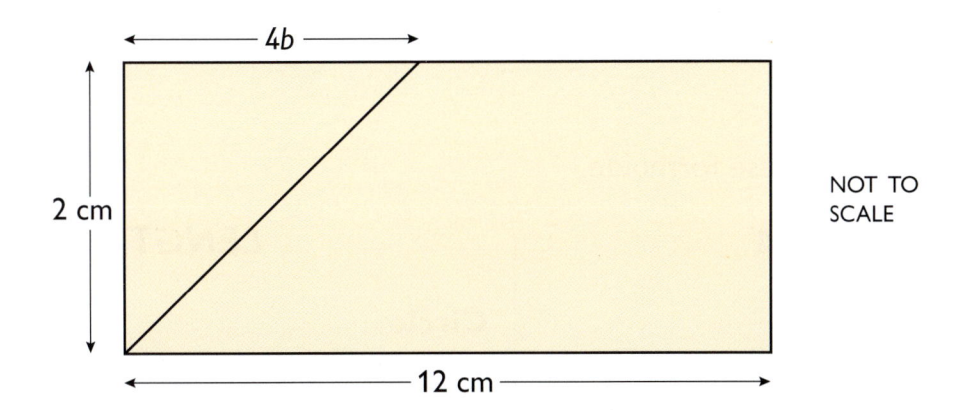

NOT TO SCALE

- 4b
- 2 cm
- 12 cm

c Find the value of *b*.

b = ... cm

d Calculate the area of the trapezium in centimetres.

Area of trapezium = ... cm²

Paper 2
Calculator Paper

You *can* use a calculator for any questions in Paper 2.

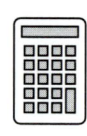

Formulae

You might need to use these formulae.

AREA

Circle

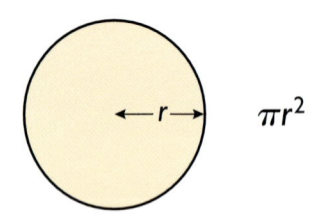

πr^2

Take π as 3.14 or use the π button on your calculator.

Triangle

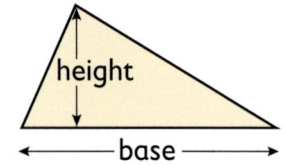

$\dfrac{\text{base} \times \text{height}}{2}$

Parallelogram

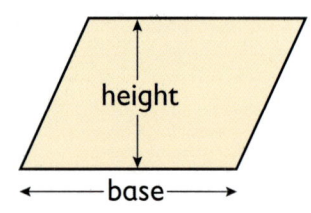

base × height

Trapezium

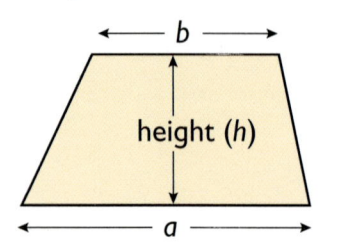

$\dfrac{(a+b)}{2} \times h$

LENGTH

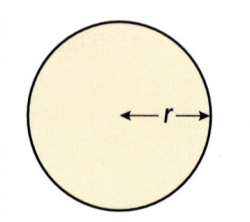

Circle

circumference = $2\pi r$

For a right-angled triangle

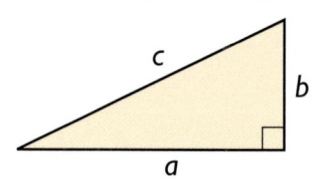

$a^2 + b^2 = c^2$ (Pythagoras' Theorem)

VOLUME

Prism

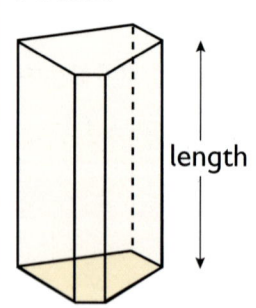

area of cross section × length

You will need:
pen, pencil, rubber, ruler, scientific or graphic calculator, protractor, tracing paper, a pair of compasses, mirror (optional).

Paper 2

Ratio

1 When making a cement **mix**, Dave follows this instruction:

| **2 parts cement** to **5 parts sand** |

a In one, Dave uses **15 kg** of **sand**.

How much cement does he use?

cement = ... kg

b In a second mix, Dave uses **8 kg** of **cement**.

How much sand does he use?

sand = ... kg

c Dave makes a third mix. He makes a total of **49 kg** of mix.

How much cement and sand does he use?

Show your working.

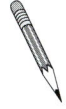

cement = ... kg   sand = ... kg

1

1

2

TOTAL

4

25

Paper 2

Vegetables

2 This graph shows the height above ground level of two vegetable plants grown from seeds over an eight-week period.

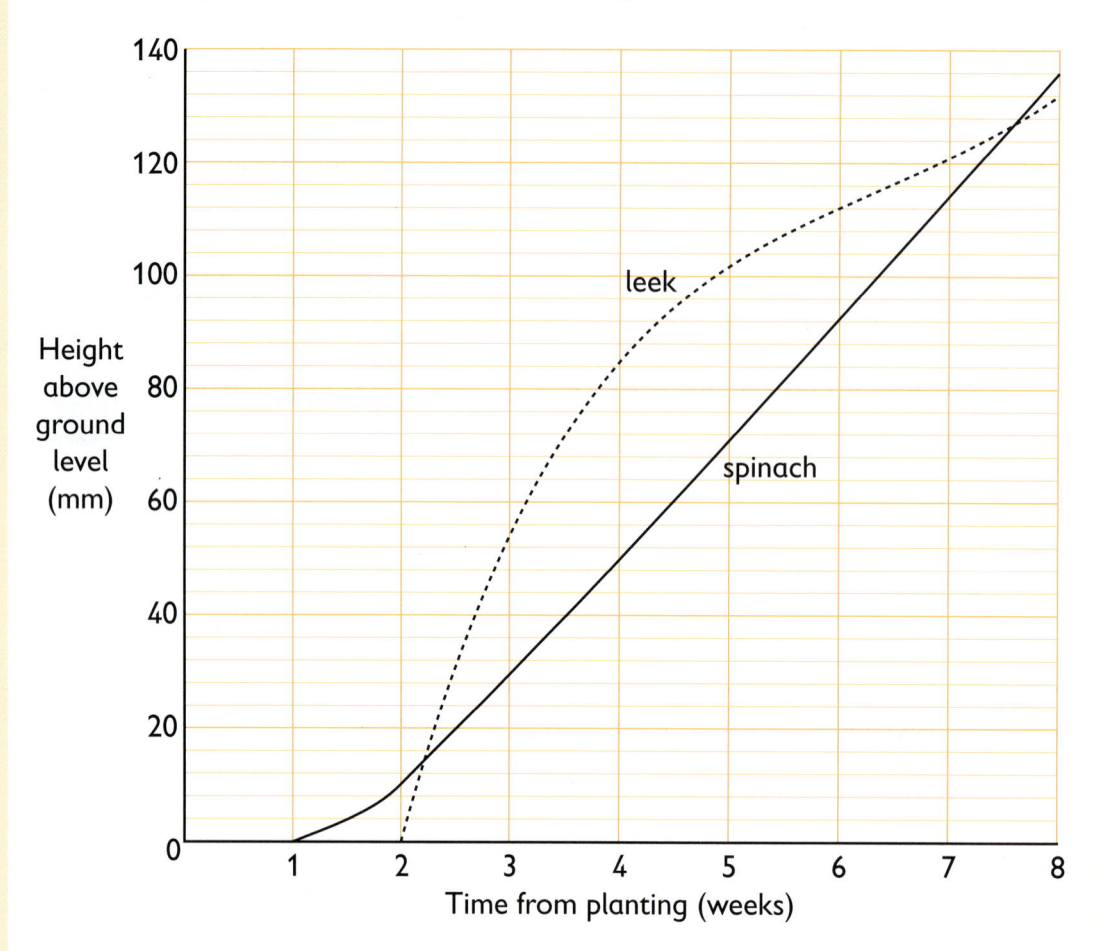

Height above ground level (mm) vs Time from planting (weeks)

a This table shows the growth of the **leek** during two-week periods. Complete the table, using the graph above.

Weeks	height at start (mm)	height at end (mm)	growth (mm)
0-2	0	0	0
2-4	0	84	84
4-6			
6-8			

This table shows the growth of the **spinach** during two-week periods.

Weeks	height at start (mm)	height at end (mm)	growth (mm)
0-2	0	0	0
2-4	10	50	40
4-6	50	92	42
6-8	92	136	44

b Use the two tables to help you describe the differences in growth rates between the two plants over the eight-week period.

Paper 2

Shape sequences

3 Here is a sequence of shapes made from white and coloured squares.

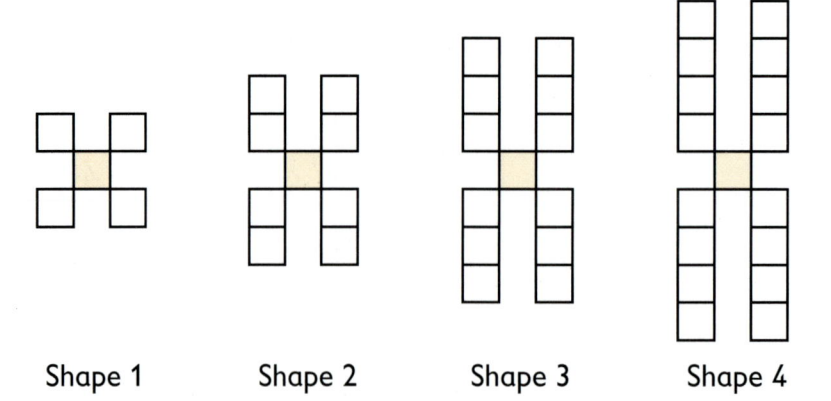

Shape 1   Shape 2   Shape 3   Shape 4

> The rule for finding the **number of squares** in **Shape n** is
> $4n + 1$

a Paul says:

"You can see that the pattern is 4n + 1 by looking at the shapes."

Explain what you think Paul means, in your own words.

b How many **white** squares and how many **coloured** squares will be in Shape 11?

.... white and   .... coloured squares

28

c Shape 3 is made from 13 squares. A shape in this sequence is made from **101** squares. What is the number of this shape?

Shape ....

d Here is a new sequence of shapes made from white and coloured squares.

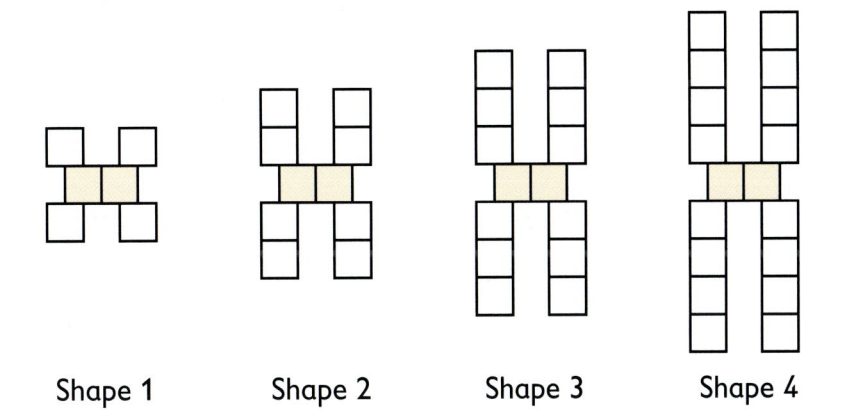

Shape 1   Shape 2   Shape 3   Shape 4

Write a rule for finding the number of squares in **Shape n.**

Number of squares =

Paper 2

Accurate drawing

4 This sketch shows the measurements of a scalene triangle. Angle *a* is not given.

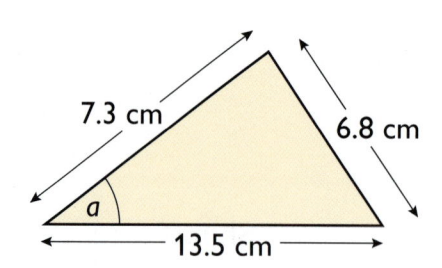

7.3 cm   6.8 cm
a
13.5 cm

a Make an **accurate** drawing of the triangle.
You may use a ruler and a pair of compasses.

b Use a protractor to measure angle *a* to the nearest degree.

a = ...°

30

5 The ages of people at two different football matches have been recorded and presented in these pie charts.

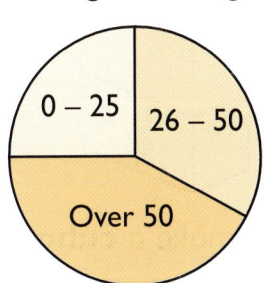

Rangers v City
0 – 25
26 – 50
Over 50

Athletic v United
Over 50
26 – 50
0 – 25

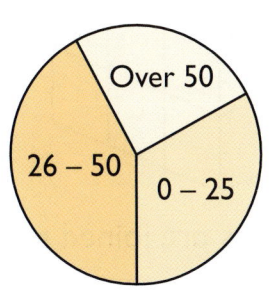

There were **24000** people at the Rangers/City match and **18000** at the Athletic/United match.

a Approximately what **percentage** of the people at the Rangers/City match were aged between **0 and 25**?

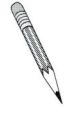

.... %

b Use your percentage to estimate the number of people at the Rangers/City match that were aged between 0 and 25.

.... people

c Compare the approximate number of people **aged 26 to 50** at **both** matches.

There were about .... 26 to 50 year-olds at Rangers/City.

There were about .... 26 to 50 year-olds at Athletic/United.

Paper 2

3D shapes

6 Here are two shapes made from small cubes. Both are made from a single layer of cubes. Three of the cubes are coloured.

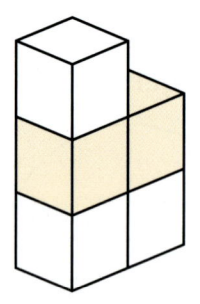

The two shapes are joined together to make a **cuboid**.

a Draw a picture of this cuboid on the dotted grid below. Shade the three coloured cubes on your picture.

b Each small cube is one centimetre cubed (1 cm³).

Write the dimensions of the cuboid you have drawn.

Length = ... cm   Width = ... cm   Height = ... cm

2

1

TOTAL

3

32

Here is a drawing of a different cuboid made from centimetre cubes.

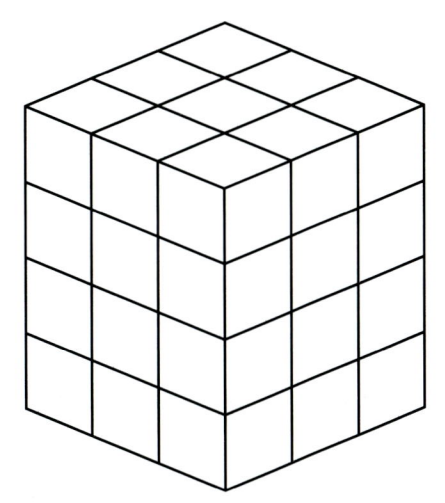

c What is the **volume** of this cuboid?

Volume = ... cm³

Chloe picks up this cuboid. She looks at it from all angles. She realises that some of the small cubes inside the cuboid cannot be seen from any angle.

d How many of the small cubes **cannot** be seen?

e What **fraction** of the total number of cubes **can** be seen?

Paper 2

Rates of exchange

7 The exchange rates for different countries are shown below.

> £1 = 3.20 German Marks
> £1 = 160 Japanese Yen

a Use the exchange rates above to find how much **80p** is in **German Marks**. You must show your working.

80p = ... German Marks

b Use the exchange rates above to find how much **752 Japanese Yen** are in **pounds**. You must show your working.

752 Japanese Yen = £ ....

c Use the exchange rates above to find how much **1 German Mark** is in **Japanese Yen**. You must show your working.

1 German Mark = ... Japanese Yen

TOTAL 6

34

8 Sandeep knows that the volume of a cuboid is **247.68 cm³**.

He knows that the height is 8 cm, and that the length is **5 cm greater** than the width.

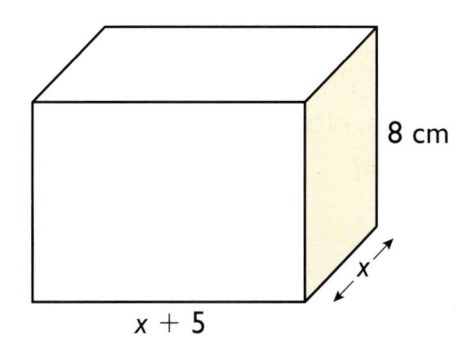

Sandeep writes this equation to show the volume of the cuboid:

$$x(x + 5) \times 8 = 247.68$$

Find the value of x.

You may find this table helpful.

x	x + 5	x (x + 5)	x (x + 5) × 8	
4	9	36	288	too large

x = ... cm

Paper 2

Offenders

9 a Read this statement.

> In 1997, **0.02%** of all 70-year-old women in England and Wales were convicted of, or cautioned for, a crime.

In 1997 there were approximately **235000** women aged 70 in England and Wales. How many were convicted of, or cautioned for, a crime?

b In the same year there were approximately **255500** men aged 60 in England and Wales. **511** of them were convicted of, or cautioned for, a crime. Write this figure as a percentage.

	Men aged 45	Women aged 45
Total number in England and Wales	330000	330000
Number convicted of, or cautioned for, a crime.	2343	561

c Use the table above to calculate the **difference** between the percentages of 45-year-old men and 45-year-old women convicted of, or cautioned for, a crime.

Paper 2

Circles

10 a The radius of a circle is 12 cm.

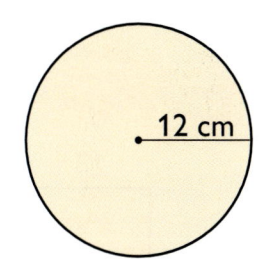

12 cm

Find the **circumference** of this circle.

Give your answer to 1 decimal place.

Show your working.

Circumference of circle = ... cm

2

b The **area** of a different circle is **531 cm^2** to the nearest centimetre.

Find the radius of this circle.

Give your answer to the nearest centimetre.

Show your working.

Radius of circle = ... cm

2

TOTAL

4

Paper 2

Grouped data

11 Some students were given a test with 49 questions and their results shown below.

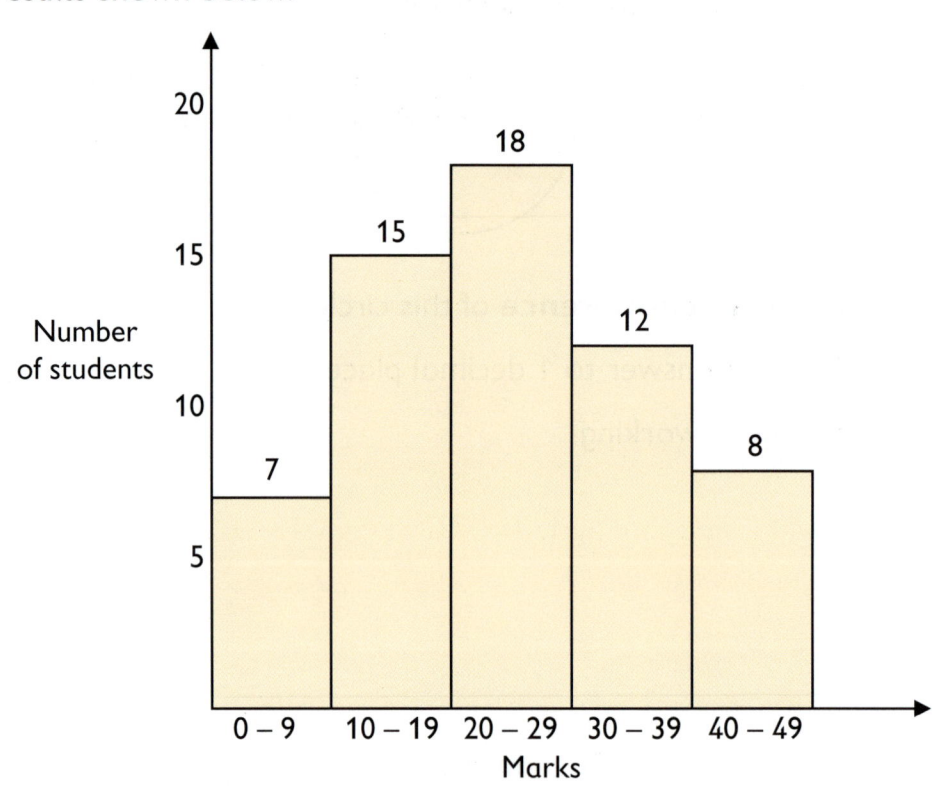

[Bar chart: Number of students vs Marks
- 0–9: 7
- 10–19: 15
- 20–29: 18
- 30–39: 12
- 40–49: 8]

a How many students took the test?

b Savo says:

"More than half of the students got below 24 marks out of 49."

Do you think Savo's comment is true or false, or do you think more information is needed? Explain your answer.

c Julie says:

"The range of the marks is 49."

Do you think Julie's comment is true or false, or do you think more information is needed? Explain your answer.

d Calculate an estimate of the **mean** mark.

You may find this table helpful. Give your answer to the nearest mark.

Marks	Midpoint of bar (x)	Number of students (f)	fx
0–9	4.5	7	31.5
10–19	14.5	15	
20–29	24.5	18	
30–39	34.5	12	
40–49	44.5	8	

.... marks

e Write your answer to part (d) as a percentage of the total marks in the test. Give your answer to 3 significant figures.

.... %

Paper 2

Simultaneous equations

12 Petra and Ed have different amounts of money in whole pounds.

Call the number of pounds Petra has x and the number of pounds Ed has y.

If you multiply Petra's amount by four and then subtract five, you get Ed's amount.

If you multiply Petra's amount by three and then add five, you get twice Ed's amount.

Use these statements to write two simultaneous equations and solve them.

Show your working.

$x =$ .... $y =$ ....

4

TOTAL

4

13 Calvin, a painter, uses a clean, straight stirring stick for mixing paint.

He slowly pushes the stirring stick into a paint tin as far as it will go and leans the stick against the edge of the tin.

The paint tin is cylindrical with a radius of 6 cm and a height of 20 cm.

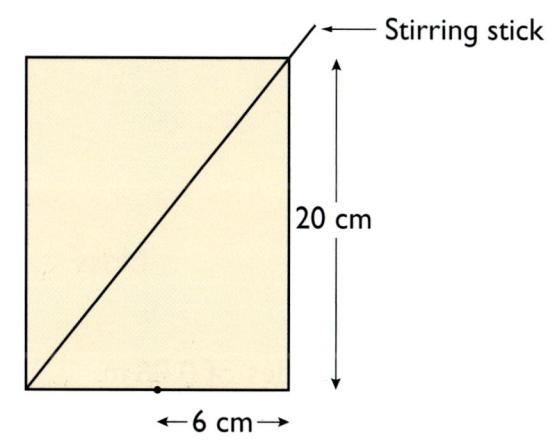

Stirring stick

20 cm

← 6 cm →

Assuming that the tin is filled to the top with paint, calculate the length of the stick that is now covered with paint.

Show your working. Give your answer to 2 significant figures.

Paper 2

Density

14 A scientist is calculating the density of a cubic object, using this formula.

$$\text{density} = \frac{\text{mass}}{\text{volume}}$$

The scientist needs to know the mass in **grams** (g) and volume in **centimetres cubed** (cm³)

a The object has a mass of **4 pounds (lb)**.

If **1 pound (lb)** is approximately equivalent to **454 grams**, what is the mass of the object in grams?

Mass = ... g

b The object is a cube with sides of 0.06 m.

Calculate the volume of the cube in centimetres cubed (cm³).

Volume = ... cm³

c Use your answers to (a) and (b) to find the density of this cube in grams per centimetre cubed (g/cm³)

Give your answer to 3 significant figures.

Density = ... g/cm³

Mental Maths Test
Questions

"For this first set of questions you have five seconds to work out each answer and write it down."

1. Write nought point six as a fraction.
2. One third of a number is four point two. What is the number?
3. How many metres are there in three and a half kilometres?
4. If I pick a ball, at random, from a full set of snooker balls, the probability that I pick a red ball is fifteen over twenty one. What is the probability that I don't pick a red ball?
5. What is six hundred and forty divided by ten?
6. Change the expression on the answer sheet into its simplest form.

"For the next set of questions you have ten seconds to work out each answer and write it down."

7. The time is twenty five past six in the evening. How many minutes is this before eighteen forty five?
8. What percentage is thirty seven out of fifty?
9. Look at the answer sheet. What is the volume of the cuboid?
10. The probability that a dice will show a five when rolled is one sixth. If sixty dice are rolled, how many dice would you expect to show a five?
11. Look at the answer sheet. What is the value of the expression when c equals five?
12. Subtract five point four from eight point one.
13. A bath has a capacity of ninety litres. About how many gallons is this?
14. Look at the answer sheet. What is the value of eight y?
15. Write two numbers with a difference of two point five.
16. Look at the answer sheet. Use the calculation given to find the answer to three hundred and forty four divided by sixteen.
17. Eighty per cent of a box of twenty tiles were broken. How many were broken?
18. Look at the answer sheet. What is the perimeter of the rectangle?

Mental Maths Test

"For the next set of questions you have fifteen seconds to work out each answer and write it down."

19 Write two numbers with a sum of seventeen and a difference of two.

20 Look at the answer sheet. What is the size of the missing angle?

21 Floor tiles are fifty centimetres long and fifty centimetres wide. How much floor will eight tiles cover?

22 What is one hundred and forty divided by five?

23 Look at the answer sheet. Write an approximate answer to the question.

24 Look at the answer sheet. The lengths of three pieces of wood are shown. You cut these lengths from a plank two metres long. How long is the plank now?

25 What is four to the power four divided by sixteen?

26 A triangle has two internal angles of forty nine degrees and fifty three degrees. What is the size of the third angle?

27 Look at the answer sheet. Draw a ring around the smallest number.

28 Look at the answer sheet. This snooker table measures twelve feet by six feet. What would be the area of a snooker table with sides half as long?

29 What is nineteen multiplied by eleven?

30 There are thirty six books on a shelf. There are five times as many paperback books as hardback books. How many hardback books are on the shelf?

Mental Maths Test
Answer Sheets

5-second questions

1. ☐

2. ☐ 4.2

3. ☐ m

4. ☐ 15/21

5. ☐

6. ☐ a × a

10-second questions

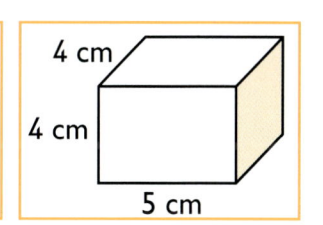

7. ☐ minutes

8. ☐ %

9. ☐ cm³   [cuboid: 4 cm × 4 cm × 5 cm]

10. ☐ 1/6

1
1
1
1
1
1

1
1
1
1

TOTAL
10

45

Mental Maths Test

| 11 | | 3c + 2 |

| 12 | | 5.4   8.1 |

| 13 | gallons |

| 14 | | 12y = 36 |

| 15 | |

| 16 | | 688 ÷ 16 = 43 |

| 17 | |

| 18 | cm | 7.5 cm area = 37.5 cm² |

15-second questions

| 19 | and |

| 20 | ° | 65° 37.5°

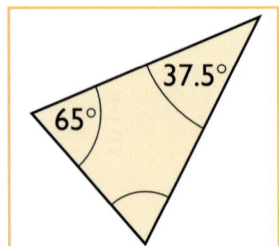

TOTAL 10

46

Mental Maths Test

21

22

23 71.9 × 7.06

24 lengths of wood
53 cm   80 cm   47 cm

25

26

27 2.54   2.45   3.0   2.5   2.52

28 feet^2 6 feet   12 feet

29

30

Answers

Paper 1

Question number	Answer	Mark	Comments and tips
Practice questions	$\frac{3}{8}$ $\frac{3}{4}$	–	You cannot use calculators for any of the questions in Paper 1. You can work answers out anywhere on the page or you can work answers out mentally. For some questions you might gain a mark for your written working out even if you get the answer wrong.
Fractions and percentages			
1a	$\frac{3}{10}$	1	Three out of ten pieces of chocolate have been eaten.
1b	$\frac{1}{5}$ 80%	1 1	Two out of ten pieces of chocolate have been eaten. $\frac{2}{10}$ is the same value as $\frac{1}{5}$. Eight out of ten pieces have not been eaten. $\frac{8}{10}$ is the same value as $\frac{80}{100}$ which is 80%.
1c	Six of the squares should be shaded.	1	$\frac{6}{10}$ is the same value as $\frac{3}{5}$
1d	Six of the squares should be shaded.	1	30% is the same value as $\frac{30}{100}$ which is $\frac{3}{10}$ This means that for every ten squares three should be shaded, totalling six out of twenty.
Money			
2a	£2.50	1	Note that amounts should never be written with both the **£** sign and a **p** sign, e.g. £2.50p
2b	£19.20	1	Any written or mental method can be used.
2c	20	1	Again, any written or mental method can be used.
Tiles			
3a		1	You might want to use a small mirror to check your solution.
3b		1	You might want to use a small mirror to check your solution.
3c		2	You might want to use a small mirror to check your solution. If one or two squares are incorrectly shaded, 1 mark should be awarded.

Paper 1 Answers

Question number	Answer	Mark	Comments and tips
Co-ordinates			
4a	(1, 2) (1,6) (2,7) (3,7) (3,4) (2,4) These sets of co-ordinates can be in any order.	1	Remember that the *x* co-ordinate is the first co-ordinate and tells you how many **across** to travel from 0. The *y* co-ordinate comes second and tells you how many **up** to travel from 0. (1,2) means across 1 and up 2.
4b	(4, 2) (4,6) (5,7) (6,7) (6,4) (5,4) (in any order)	1	The phrase '*x* is a cross: *x* is across' can help you to remember.
4c	Shape B is the same as Shape A but has been moved (translated) across (to the right) three places.	1	If you add something to all the *x* co-ordinates the shape appears to move to the right. If you subtract from all the *x* co-ordinates the shape appears to move to the left.
4d	The shape would appear to move down two places.	1	If you add something to all the *y* co-ordinates the shape appears to move up. If you subtract from all the *y* co-ordinates it appears to move down.
Missing numbers			
5(a–e)	10 4 142 40 72 1 mark for each	5	Always look at the finished equation when you have written a missing number to see if it makes sense. For the question $\boxed{} \div 6 = 12$, if you *incorrectly* divided 12 by 6 and wrote the missing number 2, you would see that $\boxed{2} \div 6$ doesn't equal 12!
Multiplying			
6a	23 20 3 10 | 200 | 30 | 230 16 6 | 120 | 18 | 138 — 368 Area of rectangle = 368 cm²	3	If most of the diagram is correct, but the final answer is incorrect, you get two marks.
Chocolate box			
7a	$\frac{1}{2}$	1	There are 30 chocolates. The probability of picking a dark chocolate is 15 out of 30. $\frac{15}{30}$ is the same value as $\frac{1}{2}$
7b	(mark at 1/6 on line)	1	There are 30 chocolates. The probability of picking a white chocolate is 5 out of 30. $\frac{5}{30}$ is the same value as $\frac{1}{6}$ Note that $\frac{1}{6}$ can be marked on the line by splitting the whole line into 6 equal parts.
7c	(mark at 2/3 on line)	1	There are 30 chocolates. The probability of picking a milk chocolate is 10 out of 30, so the probability of not picking one is 20 out of 30. $\frac{20}{30}$ is the same value as $\frac{2}{3}$ or $\frac{4}{6}$
7d	The third statement only should be ticked	1	There are still 14 dark chocolates out of the 29 left. $\frac{14}{29}$ is a greater probability than $\frac{5}{29}$ (white) or $\frac{10}{29}$ (milk)

Paper 1 Answers

Question number	Answer	Mark	Comments and tips
Film processing			
8a	$3n$	1	The answers $n \times 3$ or $3 \times n$ are acceptable, but it is better to shorten the expression to $3n$.
8b	$n \div 2$ or $\frac{1}{2}n$ or $\frac{n}{2}$	1	Any of these three expressions are acceptable, but the second two are preferable.
8c	$1\frac{1}{2}n$ or $\frac{3}{2}n$ or $n + \frac{1}{2}n$	1	
Negatives			
9a	8	1	Imagine a number line, e.g. $^-3\ ^-2\ ^-1\ 0\ 1\ 2\ 3\ 4\ 5$ Starting at $^-3$ you need to count on 8 to reach the number 5.
9b	4	1	$6 - 8 = ^-2$. To reach 2 from $^-2$ you need to count on 4.
9c	$^-7$	1	$5 + ^-2 = 3$. To go from 3 to $^-4$ you must add $^-7$.
9d	$^-4 + ^-5 - 1$ or $^-5 + ^-4 - 1$ or $^-4 - 1 + ^-5$ or $^-5 - 1 + ^-4$	1	
Profits			
10a	True False False True	2	1 mark if one answer is incorrect.
10b	£4000	1	The range can be found by subtracting the lowest value from the highest, e.g. £4500 − £500.
10c	September's bar should be drawn in to the value of £1500.	1	The mean value (£1000) is the total of all the values divided by 6 (the number of months).
10d	£1500	1	The mean value of the first six months is £2000. This can be found by adding all the values to get £12000 and dividing by 6 (the number of months). The second part of the year has a mean of £1000, so the mean over the whole year is £1500.
Triangles			
11a	$a = 95°$ $b = 85°$ $c = 30°$	3	Angle a is the same as the 95° angle as there are 2 parallel lines with the line PQ crossing both of them. Imagine the 95° angle sliding along line PQ until it sits on top of angle a. You will see that they are the same. Angle b is found by subtracting 95° from 180° (angles on a straight line). The angles inside a triangle add up to 180°. Therefore angle c can be found by adding 95 and 55 and subtracting this from 180°.
11b	6 cm	1	If the larger triangle has sides twice the length of the smaller triangle then point T must be the midpoint of the line PR. Thus if TR is 6 cm, then PT must also be 6 cm.

Paper 1 Answers

Question number	Answer	Mark	Comments and tips
Sequences			
12a	11	1	
12b	5 7 19 All three numbers must be correct.	1	You will see that the number of hexagons in a layer is always one less than the layer number multiplied by two.
12c	$2n - 1$	1	
Equations			
13a	$x = 11$ $y = 7$ $z = 8$ 1 mark each	3	$3x - 10 = 23$, so $3x = 23 + 10 = 33$ If $3x = 33$, then x must be 11. $4y + 20 = 48$, so $4y = 48 - 20 = 28$ If $4y = 28$, then y must be 7. $z^2 - 6 = 58$, so $z^2 = 58 + 6 = 64$ If $z^2 = 64$ then z must be 8.
13b	$w = 25$ cm 1 mark for showing the expression $4w + 10$ in your working.	2	The perimeter is the distance all the way around the edge of the shape. The perimeter therefore is $w + 5 + w + w + 5 + w = 4w + 10$. So 110 cm (the perimeter given) $= 4w + 10$ $4w + 10 = 110$, so $4w = 110 - 10 = 100$ If $4w = 100$, w must be 25.
Fractions			
14a	12 $\frac{1}{9}$ $\frac{1}{3}$ 18 $\frac{1}{2}$ 27 $\frac{3}{4}$ 9	5	1 mark given for each correct fraction. 1 mark given for all the other numbers correct.
Areas of shapes			
15a	9 cm²	1	Area of a triangle $= \frac{1}{2}(b \times h)$ Area $= \frac{1}{2}(4.5 \times 4) = \frac{1}{2}(18) = 9$
15b	Area = 25 cm² 1 mark given for using the equation area $= \frac{(a+b)}{2} \times h$ even if answer is incorrect.	2	Area of trapezium $= \frac{(a+b)}{2} \times h$. area $= \frac{(4 + 8.5)}{2} \times 4 = 25$
15c	2 cm	1	Area of a triangle $= \frac{1}{2}(b \times h)$ Area $= \frac{1}{2}(4b \times 2) = \frac{1}{2}(8b) = 4b$ If 8 cm $= 4b$, then $b = 2$
15d	Area = 16 cm²	1	Area of trapezium $= \frac{(a+b)}{2} \times h$. area $= \frac{(4 + 12)}{2} \times 2 = 16$

Answers

Paper 2

Question number	Answer	Mark	Comments and tips
Ratio			
1a	6 kg	1	The ratio is 2 parts cement for every 5 parts sand. We can write this as the ratio 2:5. If there is 15 kg of sand (three times the number in the ratio) then cement must be three times the *other* number in the ratio, i.e. $2 \times 3 = 6$.
1b	20 kg	1	If there is 8 kg of cement (four times the number in the ratio) then sand must be four times *the other* number in the ratio, i.e. $4 \times 5 = 20$
1c	14 kg and 35 kg 1 mark each	2	In the ratio 2:5, there are a total of 7 parts. If a total of 49 kg is mixed (seven times the ratio total) then both cement and sand must be seven times their numbers in the ratio.
Vegetables			
2a	84 112 28 112 132 20 1 mark for each row	2	Each interval is worth 4 mm.
2b	Your explanation should include the fact that for the leek the growth rate slowed and for the spinach the growth rate increased.	2	Other differences include the fact that the leek was later in reaching ground level, but grew much more quickly between 2 and 4 weeks.
Shape sequences			
3a	Your explanation should show that you have noticed that the central coloured square in each shape is represented by +1 and the 4n represents the four 'legs' on each shape.	1	
3b	44 and 1	1	The rule is $4n + 1$. For shape 11, $n = 11$ so $4n + 1 = (4 \times 11) + 1 = 44$ and 1.
3c	25	1	The rule is $4n + 1$. If $4n + 1 = 101$, then $4n = 101 - 1 = 100$ If $4n = 100$, then n must be 25.
3d	$4n + 2$	1	There are 2 central coloured squares (+2) and 4 'legs' ($4n$), so the total number is $4n + 2$. The equations $2 + 4n$ or $(4 \times n) + 2$ are also acceptable.

52

Paper 2 Answers

Question number	Answer	Mark	Comments and tips
Accurate drawing			
4a	To check your answer, measure the perpendicular height of your triangle. If the height is exactly 2.2 cm then you score 2 marks. If the height is between 2.1 cm and 2.3 cm you score 1 mark.	2	
4b	17°	1	
Charts			
5a	25%	1	One quarter is the same value as 25%.
5b	6000	1	25% of 24000 or one quarter of 24000 can be found by dividing 24000 by 4 = 6000.
5c	8000 7500 1 mark each	2	Approximately one third of 24000 = 8000. Approximately five twelfths of 18000 = 7500.
3D shapes			
6a	A cuboid accurately drawn, e.g. with 3 coloured cubes correctly positioned. The cuboid can be drawn in a different orientation.	2	These solutions are acceptable. 1 mark if coloured cubes are not correctly shaded.
6b	2 cm 1 cm 5 cm *or* 2 cm 5 cm 1 cm *or* 1 cm 2 cm 5 cm *or* 1 cm 5 cm 2 cm *or* 5 cm 1 cm 2 cm *or* 5 cm 2 cm 1 cm	1	The order of the dimensions will depend on the orientation of the shape you have drawn.
6c	36 cm³	2	The volume of a cuboid is found by multiplying the length by the width by the height: $3 \times 3 \times 4 = 36$ cm³
6d	2	1	
6e	$\frac{34}{36}$ or $\frac{17}{18}$	1	If two cannot be seen then 34 (36 minus 2) can be seen. 34 out of a total of 36 is written as a fraction as $\frac{34}{36}$.
Rates of exchange			
7a	2.56	2	Divide 3.2 German Marks by 100 to find how many Marks are the same as 1 pence. Then multiply by 80.
7b	£4.70. You do not get an answer for writing £4.07 or £4.7.	2	Divide 752 Yen by 160 to find how many pounds they are equivalent to.
7c	50	2	Divide 160 Yen by 3.2 to find how many Yen are equivalent to one German Mark.

Paper 2 Answers

Question number	Answer	Mark	Comments and tips
Expressions			
8	$x = 3.6$ cm	3	
Offenders			
9a	47	1	$235000 \times 0.02 \div 100 = 47$
9b	0.2%	1	511 men out of 255500 can be written as the fraction 511/255500 and multiplied by 100 to find the percentage.
9c	0.54% 1 mark for showing the percentages 0.71 and 0.17	2	2343 men out of 330000 can be written as the fraction 2343/33000 and multiplied by 100 to find the percentage = 0.71. 561 women out of 330000 can be written as the fraction 561/33000 and multiplied by 100 to find the percentage = 0.17. The difference is found by subtracting 0.17 from 0.71.
Circles			
10a	75.4 cm 1 mark for an answer such as 75.36 cm or 75.3 cm.	2	The circumference of a circle is $2\pi r$ or πd. $d = 24$ cm, therefore the circumference $= 24\pi$.
10b	13 cm	2	The area of the circle, πr^2, is 531 cm^2 Divide 531 by π to find r^2 and then use the square root button $\sqrt{}$ on your calculator to find r.
Grouped data			
11a	60	1	Add together 7, 15, 18, 12 and 8.
11b	This graph does not give enough information about the precise scores the students got.	1	Within the group 20-29 all the students could have scored 29 marks, in which case Savo is wrong, or scored 20, in which case he is right.
11c	Again, we need more information.	1	The range of a set of data is found by subtracting the lowest value from the highest value.
11d	24 marks 1 mark for 24.3 marks or 24.333…	2	The total value for fx should be divided by 60 (the number of students) to find the mean value. This should be given to the nearest whole mark.
11e	49.0%	1	24 divided by 49 multiplied by 100. The answer 49 would not score a mark.
Simultaneous equations			
12	$x = £3$ $y = £7$ 1 mark for each. 2 marks if these equations are shown: $4x - 5 = y$ $3x + 5 = 2y$	4	There are different methods for solving simultaneous equations. One example is shown below: Multiply each value in the equation $4x - 5 = y$ by 2 To give $8x - 10 = 2y$. Subtract $3x + 5 = 2y$ from this equation. $5x - 15 = 0$, therefore $5x = 15$, so x must equal 3. If $x = 3$ and $4x - 5 = y$, then $12 - 5 = y$. So y must be 7.

Paper 2 Answers

Question number	Answer	Mark	Comments and tips
Paint			
13a	23 cm Score only 2 marks if your answer has more than 2 digits and starts with 23, eg 23.32 or 23.3.	3	Use Pythagoras' Theorem ($a^2 + b^2 = c^2$). $20^2 + 12^2 = x^2$ so $x^2 = 544$, therefore $x = 23.3238$ cm
Density			
14a	1816 g	1	454×4.
14b	216 cm³	1	0.06 m is 6 cm, so the volume is $6 \times 6 \times 6 = 216$ cm³.
14c	8.41 g/cm³ Score one mark for the answer 8.4 g/cm³ Your answer must have exactly three digits.	2	$1816 \div 216 = 8.407407\ldots$

Answers

Mental Maths Test

1. $\frac{3}{5}$ (accept equivalents e.g. $\frac{6}{10}$)
2. 12.6
3. 3500
4. $\frac{6}{21}$
5. 64
6. a^2
7. 20 minutes
8. 74%
9. 80 cm^3
10. 10
11. 17
12. 2.7
13. approx. 20 gallons
14. 24
15. any two numbers with a difference of 2.5 e.g. 1 and 3.5
16. 21.5
17. 16
18. 25 cm
19. 9.5 and 7.5
20. 77.5°
21. 2 m^2
22. 28
23. approx. 504
24. 20 cm
25. 16
26. 78°
27. 2.45
28. 18 feet^2
29. 209
30. 6

1 mark per correct answer

National Curriculum Levels

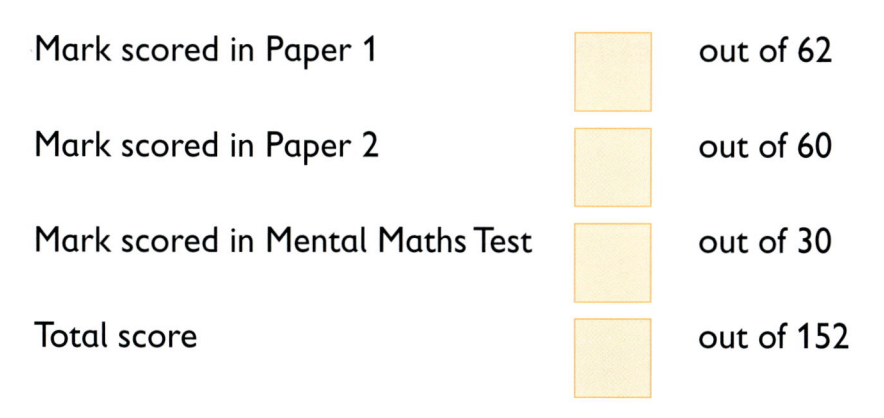

Mark scored in Paper 1   ☐   out of 62

Mark scored in Paper 2   ☐   out of 60

Mark scored in Mental Maths Test   ☐   out of 30

Total score   ☐   out of 152

Use this table to find what level you might be working at.

Mark	0–20	21–40	41–80	81–120	121–140	141–152
Level	Level 3	Level 4	Level 5	Level 6	Level 7	Level 8

If you scored over 140 marks you might want to try the Level 8 Extension Paper on the next few pages.

If you need more practice in any Maths topics, use the WH Smith Key Stage 3 Maths Revision Guide.

Extension Paper

Level 8

1 **Do NOT use a calculator for this question.**

This diagram shows a rectangle, ABCD. It is not drawn to scale.

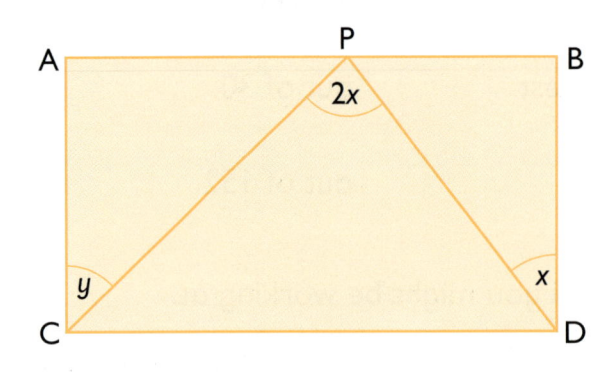

The line AB has point P along its length.
The line CP is the same length as the line CD.

a Calculate the values of x and y.

You must show your working.

$x =$ ....° $y =$ ....°

b What can you now say about triangle CPD?

Volume

Extension Paper

2 **You MAY use a calculator for this question.**

A small cone is cut from the top of a larger symmetrical cone.

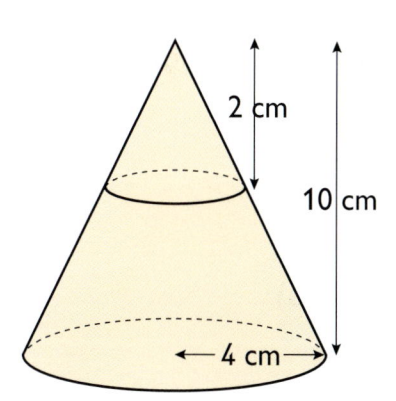

The radius of the larger cone is 4 cm and its vertical height is 10 cm.

The vertical height of the small cone is 2 cm.

a Calculate the radius of the smaller cone.

b Calculate the volume of the larger cone using the formula

$$\frac{1}{3}\pi r^2 h$$

Show your working.

c How many times larger is the volume of the larger cone than the smaller cone?

TOTAL 5

59

Answers

Level 8

1.
   a. $x = 30°, y = 30°$
   b. The triangle has internal angles of 60° and so must be an equilateral triangle.
2.
   a. 0.8 cm
   b. 167.55 cm^3
   c. 125 times (5 × 5 × 5)